COOKING JOURNAL
Recipe Book
for Kids

Blank Recipe Book

Speedy Publishing LLC

40 E. Main St., #1156

Newark, DE 19711

www.SpeedyPublishing.Co

Copyright 2013, Cooking Journal: Recipe Book for Kids
978-1-62884-693-5
First Printed July 10, 2013

Table of Contents

Breakfast

BREAKFAST

RECIPE:

INGREDIENTS:

-
-
-
-
-
-
-
-
-

-
-
-
-
-
-
-
-
-

DIRECTIONS:

PREPARATION TIME:

SERVINGS:

BREAKFAST

RECIPE:

INGREDIENTS:

-
-
-
-
-
-
-
-

-
-
-
-
-
-
-
-

DIRECTIONS:

PREPARATION TIME: **SERVINGS:**

BREAKFAST

RECIPE:

INGREDIENTS:

-
-
-
-
-
-
-
-
-
-

DIRECTIONS:

PREPARATION TIME:

SERVINGS:

BREAKFAST

RECIPE:

INGREDIENTS:

-
-
-
-
-
-
-
-
-

-
-
-
-
-
-
-
-
-

DIRECTIONS:

PREPARATION TIME: **SERVINGS:**

BREAKFAST

RECIPE:

INGREDIENTS:

-
-
-
-
-
-
-
-

-
-
-
-
-
-
-
-

DIRECTIONS:

PREPARATION TIME: **SERVINGS:**

BREAKFAST

RECIPE:

INGREDIENTS:

-
-
-
-
-
-
-
-
-

DIRECTIONS:

PREPARATION TIME:　　　　　　**SERVINGS:**

Appetizers

APPETIZERS

RECIPE:

INGREDIENTS:

-
-
-
-
-
-
-
-

DIRECTIONS:

PREPARATION TIME: **SERVINGS:**

APPETIZERS

RECIPE:

INGREDIENTS:

-
-
-
-
-
-
-
-

-
-
-
-
-
-
-
-

DIRECTIONS:

PREPARATION TIME: **SERVINGS:**

APPETIZERS

RECIPE:

INGREDIENTS:

DIRECTIONS:

PREPARATION TIME: **SERVINGS:**

APPETIZERS

RECIPE:

INGREDIENTS:

-
-
-
-
-
-
-
-
-

-
-
-
-
-
-
-
-
-

DIRECTIONS:

PREPARATION TIME: **SERVINGS:**

APPETIZERS

RECIPE:

INGREDIENTS:

-
-
-
-
-
-
-
-
-

-
-
-
-
-
-
-
-
-

DIRECTIONS:

PREPARATION TIME: **SERVINGS:**

Soups & Breads

SOUP & BREADS

RECIPE:

INGREDIENTS:

-
-
-
-
-
-
-
-
-

-
-
-
-
-
-
-
-
-

DIRECTIONS:

PREPARATION TIME:

SERVINGS:

SOUP & BREADS

RECIPE:

INGREDIENTS:

-
-
-
-
-
-
-
-
-

DIRECTIONS:

PREPARATION TIME: **SERVINGS:**

SOUP & BREADS

RECIPE:

INGREDIENTS:

-
-
-
-
-
-
-
-
-

-
-
-
-
-
-
-
-

DIRECTIONS:

PREPARATION TIME:

SERVINGS:

SOUP & BREADS

RECIPE:

INGREDIENTS:

-
-
-
-
-
-
-
-
-

-
-
-
-
-
-
-
-

DIRECTIONS:

PREPARATION TIME: **SERVINGS:**

SOUP & BREADS

RECIPE:

INGREDIENTS:

-
-
-
-
-
-
-
-
-

-
-
-
-
-
-
-
-
-

DIRECTIONS:

PREPARATION TIME: **SERVINGS:**

Sides & Salads

SIDES & SALADS

RECIPE:

INGREDIENTS:

-
-
-
-
-
-
-
-
-

-
-
-
-
-
-
-
-
-

DIRECTIONS:

PREPARATION TIME: **SERVINGS:**

SIDES & SALADS

RECIPE:

INGREDIENTS:

-
-
-
-
-
-
-
-
-

-
-
-
-
-
-
-
-
-

DIRECTIONS:

PREPARATION TIME: **SERVINGS:**

SIDES & SALADS

RECIPE:

INGREDIENTS:

-
-
-
-
-
-
-
-
-

DIRECTIONS:

PREPARATION TIME: **SERVINGS:**

SIDES & SALADS

RECIPE:

INGREDIENTS:

-
-
-
-
-
-
-
-
-
-
-
-
-
-
-
-
-
-

DIRECTIONS:

PREPARATION TIME: **SERVINGS:**

SIDES & SALADS

RECIPE:

INGREDIENTS:

-
-
-
-
-
-
-
-
-

-
-
-
-
-
-
-
-

DIRECTIONS:

PREPARATION TIME:　　　　　　**SERVINGS:**

Main Dishes

MAIN DISHES

RECIPE:

INGREDIENTS:

DIRECTIONS:

PREPARATION TIME: **SERVINGS:**

MAIN DISHES

RECIPE:

INGREDIENTS:

-
-
-
-
-
-
-
-
-

-
-
-
-
-
-
-
-
-

DIRECTIONS:

PREPARATION TIME: **SERVINGS:**

MAIN DISHES

RECIPE:

INGREDIENTS:

-
-
-
-
-
-
-
-
-

-
-
-
-
-
-
-
-

DIRECTIONS:

PREPARATION TIME: **SERVINGS:**

MAIN DISHES

RECIPE:

INGREDIENTS:

-
-
-
-
-
-
-
-
-

-
-
-
-
-
-
-
-
-

DIRECTIONS:

PREPARATION TIME:　　　　　　**SERVINGS:**

MAIN DISHES

RECIPE:

INGREDIENTS:

-
-
-
-
-
-
-
-
-

-
-
-
-
-
-
-
-
-

DIRECTIONS:

PREPARATION TIME:　　　　　　**SERVINGS:**

Desserts

DESSERTS

RECIPE:

INGREDIENTS:

DIRECTIONS:

PREPARATION TIME: **SERVINGS:**

DESSERTS

RECIPE:

INGREDIENTS:

-
-
-
-
-
-
-
-
-

-
-
-
-
-
-
-
-
-

DIRECTIONS:

PREPARATION TIME:

SERVINGS:

DESSERTS

RECIPE:

INGREDIENTS:

-
-
-
-
-
-
-
-

-
-
-
-
-
-
-
-

DIRECTIONS:

PREPARATION TIME: **SERVINGS:**

DESSERTS

RECIPE:

INGREDIENTS:

-
-
-
-
-
-
-
-
-

-
-
-
-
-
-
-
-
-

DIRECTIONS:

PREPARATION TIME: **SERVINGS:**

DESSERTS

RECIPE:

INGREDIENTS:

-
-
-
-
-
-
-
-

DIRECTIONS:

PREPARATION TIME: **SERVINGS:**

Bonus

BONUS

RECIPE:

INGREDIENTS:

-
-
-
-
-
-
-
-
-

DIRECTIONS:

PREPARATION TIME: **SERVINGS:**

BONUS

RECIPE:

INGREDIENTS:

-
-
-
-
-
-
-
-
-

-
-
-
-
-
-
-
-
-

DIRECTIONS:

PREPARATION TIME: **SERVINGS:**

BONUS

RECIPE:

INGREDIENTS:

-
-
-
-
-
-
-
-
-

DIRECTIONS:

PREPARATION TIME: **SERVINGS:**

BONUS

RECIPE:

INGREDIENTS:

-
-
-
-
-
-
-
-
-

-
-
-
-
-
-
-
-
-

DIRECTIONS:

PREPARATION TIME:

SERVINGS:

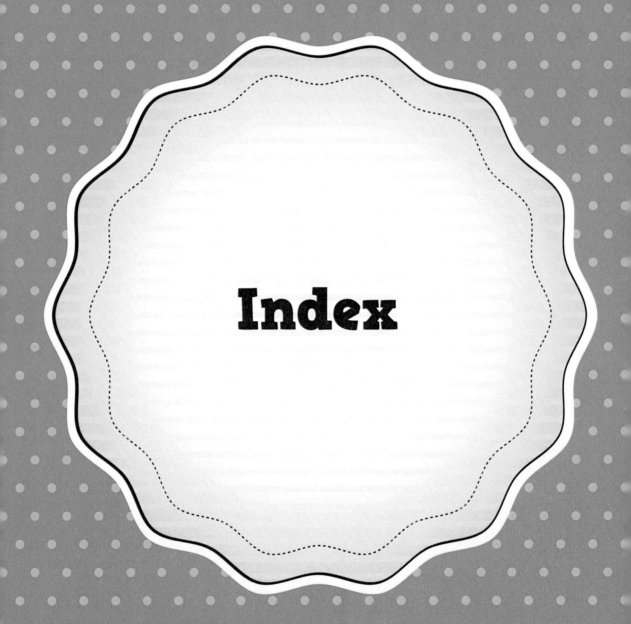

Index

INDEX

A   pg

B

C

D

E

F

G

H

I

J

INDEX

K   pg

L

M

N

O

P

Q

R

S

T

INDEX

U   pg

Z

75910027R00029

Made in the USA
San Bernardino, CA
06 May 2018